Step-by-Step Guide on How to Become a Published Author

THE NEXT UP

Kenshae Westmoreland

ISBN: 978-0-578-95180-5
Library of Congress Cataloging-in-Publication Data
Printed in the United States of America

For more information contact: Inspired by K, 615.525.7836 or email. Please include your email and phone number.

Email: Inspiredbykw@gmail.com
Website: www.inspiredbyktheblog.com

Editor: Tracy Johnson, Proof Your Point
Cover Designer: Joseph Okerentie (icra8design@gmail.com)
Book Layout and Design: Joseph Okerentie (icra8design@gmail.com)
Book Publishing Coach: Renee Bobb

Dedication

This book is dedicated to those who want to turn their dreams into reality by becoming an author. I want to share valuable information and show young ladies that anything is possible.

Acknowledgments

I would like to take this time to thank some people who have helped me financially and emotionally throughout this book process.

My life coaches, who have supported my vision in many ways.

I am thankful for being educated by Ash Cash on this process as well as guiding me in mindset mentally.

My new mentor, Renee Bobb, who has guided me in the right direction to further my dreams.

Lastly, my family and friends, who have always believed in me. I am so thankful for you all.

Table Of Contents

Introduction

Hey, how are you today? You are here either because you want to be an author or you want to know how to get paid as an author. The self-publishing industry has grown over the years, and with technology now it is much easier. Working as a self-publisher allowed me to have control over my publications and income. You can make over four figures from your book with the right plan. Every step is critical because I know from publishing my first poetry book, *Inspired by K.*

That is why I wrote this step-by-step guide to help all aspiring authors start their passion while making an income. I have made these steps so that you can more simply understand the publishing process. Every step will be important and very detailed so that you can succeed. If you do go by this guide, your results will show as mine did! After reading this guide you will know exactly how to publish your book and how to make money from your book. Everything you need to self-publish your book is here! You are going to love it.

About The Author

Kenshae Westmoreland is a young entrepreneur with ambition. She had been in the self-publishing industry for approximately five years before releasing her first book. She is the creator of Eleven11 Publishing House, which provides self-publishers a chance to self-publish with direct guidance.

As a career, she uses her brand "Inspired by K" to motivate and empower young ladies. She provides little sisters with mental, financial, and learning support. She has trained to be able to give off positive vibrations. Inspired by K: An Inspirational Chapbook, her first book, contains poems designed to release positive waves into readers' lives.

Kenshae has won rewards for entrepreneur development from Tennessee State University, specifically for her great business plan and creativity in 2017. She graduated high school and attended some college at Nashville State. Kenshae participated in several interviews on News Channel 5 and also performed her poems on the same station for black history month in 2017.

Her passion for poetry and writing started in elementary school, where she and her friends wrote books for their book club. From there, she started with spoken words, performing black history poems on the news as well as participating in events up through high school. Her best class in college was public speaking. During senior year, her granny had an aneurysm that was about to explode. This led to several strokes and a coma. She missed her graduation physically but she felt her when she visited her in 2017. Competing in internationals for a business competition while receiving the news is what made Kenshae stronger. As her granny's recovery process made it possible to move from the nursing home to her mother's house, Kenshae was inspired to keep writing in college after losing her great-grandma and father in her freshman year. She now serves as her granny's full-time caregiver as she juggles other responsibilities with the help of her sister and mom.

Growing up with a single parent, who worked so hard in making things work just to get by, has always kept Kenshae focused. She shares her methods with young people to help them get over obstacles. She has mastered the ability to create her reality and wants to motivate and share through what God has done for her. As she says, "The same way He brought me out, He will do the same for you."

My Experience

When I wrote my first book it was poetry because poetry always has been my strongest area. A poetry book is a book of fifty or more poems. I was rejected time after time when I submitted to publishing houses. One house told me it would cost $2,500 to publish my book. I did not have that money, so I decided to research self-publishing. Amazon Kindle Direct popped up and I followed their template. I joined webinars and trainings about how to sell a book. It was very complicated because I was getting information in different ways every time.

I finally decided to just publish and forget about anything else. I missed having the plan and strategies laid out correctly, and that is what messed me up. You have to go through every step to see the results you desire to see. Self-publishing is a full-time job and if you are not ready, please let me know! This guide will be a valuable tool for you, so please read it until you understand it. This guide will make you an expert—believe me—but first I will give you my tips that will help you succeed.

1. Stay focused to remain focused: The only way to accomplish a goal you set for yourself is by staying focused. The world will give you what you ask for, but you must be clear and focused about it. Never give up when obstacles come to destroy you.

2. Keep a positive mindset: You have to always keep positive energy flowing into your life. Feed your brain affirmations and prayers. When you think positively, you will receive a positive outcome.

3. Commitment: If you have never committed to anything before, then this is it. You must commit to your goals to fulfill your dreams. Put in the work and get great results.

4. Purpose: Always keep your purpose in the front of your mind. Do the work that is required to make your purpose valuable. You must be confident in your purpose to impact others.

5. Believe: If you can believe it, you can achieve it. If you believe you are capable of writing a book, then you are! Your story is needed and the market is never full.

6. Research: Always focus on your target audience because this is very

important if you want to self-publish. Focus on your budget because you are in control of the process. Focus and research your market that you are trying to enter. Explore your options.

7.   Think bigger: The world has billions of people in it. You must dream big. Whatever you think, write it down and act on it. If you can think of it, you can do it. You must think like an entrepreneur in this industry. Expand your thinking process and plan correctly to reach customers.

8.   Ask for help: It does not hurt to get help from an expert. It helps you become an expert as well and makes you more credible. Research self-publishing to get a head start. Get familiar with holding multiple positions. If you need to hire an assistant, please do if it fits within your budget.

Now write down some things that motivate you and keep you going.

_____

_____

_____

_____

_____

_____

_____

_____

_____

_____

STEP 1:

PICKING YOUR NICHE

(WHY ARE YOU WRITING YOUR BOOK?)

Your niche is very important when writing your book because you need to target who you want to read your book. You may have many niches as you would like, but that will just make it harder to target when selling. When choosing your niche you want to know why you are targeting the niche. You want to be very clear on who you want to receive your message. Therefore, keeping your why in front of your mind at all times will serve your who.

Example: *Inspired by K: An Inspirational Chapbook* targets poetry readers, and readers who need inspiration, affirmations, and positive readings. Everyone needs that, right? However, it's a broad niche that needs to be narrowed down. So, you have to narrow it down to self-help. It points to the customer who is needing self-help.

How do you pick your niche? Great question! This is exactly what you need to do.

Write down subjects you feel strongly about as well as your weakest subjects. These subjects can be anything in general life: social issues—any opinion you have. What is something you know you are an expert at and what is something that you feel strongly about but need more background information? The subject is how you find your niche. Next, find your solutions to your weakest points using your strongest areas, and sort them out. Your weakest points are things you want to solve but need more information to solve. What subjects you can relate to the most is something you can talk about the most. Which subject have you overcome and want to share? Make sure you are confident in what you are sharing. What exactly can you offer the market? Ask yourself this question: *Would I read this book and, if so, will it benefit me after reading it?* Readers should want to share their stories after reading them. Your niche should be responsive and a problem-solving era.

- If you want to sell a massive number of books and make an impact, you must first start with your MINDSET.

- Mindset. Your mindset is your mental attitude, and your mental attitude should be confident with the information you share.

- Believing you can do it, Dreaming you can make a change, and Doing the work to achieve your goal.

- Start with affirmations out loud two times per day.

- Affirmations:

"I will become an author and make an impact."

"My story is important and people want to read it."

"I am a light source that the world needs."

"I will succeed as an author."

"My gift as an author will bring me income."

"I am confident in my story which is true."

"I will be a best-selling author."

When your mind is focused and has clarity about what it wants, you can achieve anything. The secret to creating a great book is believing you can create a great book. A strong belief requires action behind it.

You are to write these affirmations down and say them every morning and night as you work on your book. The more you write down what you believe, the more it is expected to turn into reality. There has always been a saying that if you write things down, they can get done. You cannot accomplish anything without proper action. The mind is a powerful thing, so you must feed positive words into it. You have to train your mindset to grow so that you can be a better person. This is a critical step because you need to put these vibrations into the world to succeed.

The three essentials for success:

- You must have a burning desire to inspire the world.

- You must be clear in your definite purpose.

- You must take the appropriate action.

Reading your affirmations and feeding your brain with positivity is the secret of tackling your goals. The power of the tongue is very strong. If you can believe it, you can achieve it. Now that you have found your niche and you are confident in your information, it is time to execute Step 2.

Use this space below to write down your affirmations that will help you.

_____

_____

_____

_____

_____

_____

_____

_____

_____

_____

STEP 2:
DETERMINE TRADITIONAL OR SELF-PUBLISHING

Choosing whether to publish your book with a traditional publishing company or to self-publish on your own can be a hard decision. Most people would like to publish through traditional publishing houses, but it usually takes years to finish your book. It would be great to have a publishing company associated with your name, of course, but it is not always the best course of action. You may also lose creative control under a traditional publisher. Some houses may not want to accept your manuscript. It may cost thousands of dollars to publish. On the other hand, these are some of the advantages of signing with a traditional publishing company:

1.   You will have a dedicated team behind your work to take your book to the next level. This team would consist of editors, cover designers, marketers, etc.

2.   You may receive more validation signing with a publishing company because it eliminates self-doubt and raises a positive signal that the company believes your book could be successful.

3.   You will have access to bookstores more easily due to traditional publisher relationships that have already been established.

4.   Gaining awards for your book is higher.

5.   You will be able to use their brand to expand yours.

Unlike traditional publishers, you may not make the money you intended and may have to end up marketing your book yourself. There are a ton of authors who they publish, but there is no personal connection. Self-publishing is underrated and is the way to have full ownership. Sometimes self-publishing draws red flags to readers. Some think it makes the author lose credibility in what they are writing about. No matter what people think, you can sell a million books as a self-publisher. Not only will you have full control over the book, but these are some reasons why it is better to self-publish:

1. You have all the control over the book publishing process, from writing to design.

2. You are going to get the most of your royalties because you are doing all the work.

3. You can sell your book worldwide and retain all the rights without having to share it with the publishing companies.

4. You can follow your niche all the way through because you have full control.

5. Self-publishing is stepping outside the box.

When you self-publish you are releasing your written project to the public. Yes, there is a process that you have to take as well as legal structures you need to follow. You will have to take on all the responsibilities over the entire process. You want to be the best author you can be. That is why you will need to hire an editor and a designer. The more you practice writing, the better you will get. You are an entrepreneur and now hold all titles in the publishing house.

- Accounting: You are responsible for all expenses and payroll of your book sales.

- Writer, editor, and designer: You have the full say so on how you want your book to look and sound.

- Packer/shipper: You have to fulfill orders as well if you want to sell a massive number of books.

- Marketer: You will have to promote your book 24/7 with a marketing plan.

- Business manager: You are responsible for securing your business structure and rights.

You need to determine which route you would like to take before diving into the industry. Self-publishing does not always mean to simply write a book and release it. It takes strategic methods, and that is what makes you stand out. The self-publishing industry is growing fast and you are the next published author. You are directly introduced to the online market instead of the third party. You can hire your staff based on your budget. You have full control of the whole process. The price to self-publish is lower than publishing through any traditional publishing house. They may think you are not established, but the methods I will provide you will make you established. You will be in full control of your book and will be creating a publishing company. If you are under the umbrella of a publishing company, it looks better to readers. It will be a lot of work because you will have to market your book. There are tools to help you reach your audience, but you will need to put in the background work as well. Which method do you prefer? Why?

_____

_____

_____

_____

_____

_____

_____

_____

_____

STEP 3:
NEVER SELF-PUBLISH!

You never want to self-publish your book! I know you are now confused as to why I said self-publishing was the best. This is the biggest secret in the self-publishing game.

So, when you self-publish you have to sign up for a Bowker account. This step is very important because it's the biggest secret, as I stated earlier. Bowker distributes ISBNs and barcodes. These are like your book's social security numbers. ISBN stands for International Standard Book Number. ISBNs will allow you to track and have your book validated through the state. You can purchase your ISBN at www.myidentifiers.com. Create your account on both "Bowkerlink" and "myidentifiers."

- One ISBN and one barcode cost $150

- Ten ISBNs cost $300

- Bookland EAN scanning symbol is needed for pricing your book: www.barcode-us.com

- Suppliers for more information: www.fotel.com and www.ggx.co

- LCCN: Catalog card number which helps identify your book in 20,000 libraries can be purchased here: www.pen.loc.gov/pen

- Copyright registration: www.leweb.loc.gov/

- copyright. You will need this to protect your work from being copied.

- Pricing: Research your competition on pricing and think about how your price will stand out.

You only have to purchase an ISBN one time for every book published. This will allow you to create your publishing company name. Use the publishing name instead of your own name.

Now your book will be published under the unobvious name, giving you more credibility. You do not want people to realize it is you. You must sign up on both platforms to sell a large number of books and reach many people. Now you can distribute books from your publishing company. You are now an entrepreneur, creating your own publishing company. This makes you certified to publish and distribute your book as well as future books.

Not saying it is self-published is the biggest gem.

Your publishing company needs to determine:

- Identified location

- Hours of operation

- Funding

- Business structure

- Business plan

- Print-on-demand services at:

  www.booksindemand.com

For example, my book is published under Eleven11 Publishing, which is my publishing company. It will show up as published by Eleven11 Publishing instead of merely self-published, which would cause a negative outlook on the book. This reminds me of the famous saying by Michael Rapaport, "Only a genius can play a fool." You may want to acknowledge that you are a self-publisher, but please remember you are an owner of a publishing company. Establish your business structure early.

SELF-PUBLISH through Amazon Kindle, Lulu.com, and IngramSpark.

Write your manuscript using one of these tools:

1.www.writepro.com

2. www.svsoft.com

3. www.novalearn.com

When you are publishing, you'll need to purchase a separate ISBN for each individual format of your book: print, eBook, and/or audiobook. If you are writing a series, you will need an International Standard Serial Number (ISSN) which can be purchased from the Library of Congress. Although the platforms will offer free ISBNs, they will then be registered with that site and not your entity. You want it to be under the umbrella of your entity so that you can receive all royalties. Your ISBN will allow you to be able to track your book sales and quantities. This is important because it needs to be registered with your publishing company.

What will you name your publishing company?

_____

_____

Which business structure works best for you? Sole Proprietorship, Partnership, Corporation, or a Limited Liability Company (LLC)?

_____

_____

Now that you have chosen to self-publish and have created your publishing company, you are ready to start publishing. Your mindset is clear and you are focused on your purpose. Now it is time to sell your book before you even write it.

STEP 4:

SELL YOUR BOOK BEFORE YOU WRITE IT

I f you were thinking your idea is good, that is not enough to sell a massive number of books. This is the biggest mistake authors make. You have to start showing that idea attention. Share your idea with friends, family, and even strangers. You need to get feedback before you waste your time on a useless subject. Your book has to be something that people want—or better yet—need. Your book has to hold a lot of value. You need to make sure your book sells before you release it by:

1.   Targeting your audience to about 100,000 or more readers.

2.   Researching your topic so much that you are an expert at what you are writing about. Look at books that fit your niche and read the reviews on them. Notice what is missing and how you can fill in the blanks.

3.   Testing your idea first to see how people respond to it. Going on Facebook Live is an engaging way to connect with people and answer questions. Ask whether it is a good idea or not and take note of the feedback you receive.

You may want to start talking about your ideal topic several months before you announce the release to build momentum for your book sales. Being clear with your audience and the problem you are solving is critical. So, once you have your entities to your book, it is now time for the title. Test the water before you jump in.

This will help you know if your book is valid or appealing.

Start the flame early by reaching out to people about your topic. Track the responses you get from family and friends. Try to reach out to strangers to get others' opinions. Your book has to hold value. It needs to be in the needy eye and not the want. You do not want to release a book about your favorite color because who does that help? Know your why and stick with your solution to that problem.

- Organize a booklet of exactly how you want your book to look. Research your niche until you are an expert in it. Research the market and ask yourself whether or not your book is marketable.

- Write your manuscript with help from Grammarly so that small grammatical errors can be checked. Organize your chapters and story plot. Create your title and subtitle. Get your finished manuscript edited.

- Be completely sure of your budget if you want to hire professionals to get the best results. Although many authors differ in their preferences, a great book includes:

1. A book cover

2. A cover page

3. A credit page

4. A dedication page

5. An acknowledgment page

6. Table of contents

7. Introduction

8. Chapters

9. About the author

10. Order form

11. A back cover and blurb

12. The spine of the book (most bookstores require a spine)

13. Author photo and bio

Credit page: The credit page is essential for readers to be able to find information about the book. At least include two or more of the following on your credit page:

1. Title and subtitle

2. Publishing company information

3. ISBN and LCCN

4. Copyright and printing rights

5. Order information

6. All contributors to the book

Dedication page: This page is used for you to dedicate your book to whomever or whatever. This is a special page for you.

Acknowledgment page: This page gives the author a chance to thank the people who have helped during the publishing process. This area is for anything for which you would like to be known.

Table of contents: This is where your chapters and page numbers can be found. This is critical to readers because it helps to find a specific chapter.

Introduction: This is important because you want to introduce your solution and address your problem. This makes it clear for readers to know what to expect.

About the author: This is the time to share any accomplishments and work ethics. This is giving the reader a chance to get to know you. You want to make sure the reader is comfortable with you and can trust you.

Order form: This is important for marketing your book. This will be a quicker way customers can share with others as to where they can find your book.

Notes:

STEP 5:

TITLE IS IMPORTANT

Your title is very important because it is the first thing that readers read. Your title needs to be short and descriptive. The best titles are memorable. You should have a subtitle following your title.

1.   Title: Something that people can remember. The title should be brief and illustrative.

2.   Subtitle: Should be long and descriptive so they know exactly what the book is going to be about.

You want to catch their attention as soon as they begin to read, so consider adding humor. Everything about your book determines how it will sell. Your title should be in the correct order of your book design. It should be clear to read and understand. You want people to feel some suspense after reading the title. They need to be interested in reading more.

The blurb is your second chance to get the reader's attention. The blurb is for the back of the book. A blurb provides the synopsis. This is where you should find what to expect in the book. Put yourself in the reader's shoes to make a perfect blurb. The title and blurb are important because this is what they will read first.

Blurb: Synopsis on the back of your book.

1.   Introduce the direct problem. Don't explain everything. Instead, set a scene.

2.   Outline how you propose to solve the problem.

3. Ask questions that will leave readers skeptical.

4. Make a promise that their lives will be better after reading.

5. Your blurb should be 250 words or less.

What will your title and subtitle be?

_____

_____

Write down your story topics.

_____

_____

_____

STEP 6:
COVER

People will indeed judge your book by its cover. That means you need to have a professional designer to design your cover. Do not design your cover yourself. Do not make your cover too busy for people to focus on the main objective. You may want to have several suggestions for your designer. Do not add NYC bestsellers if it is not credible. This will draw a huge red flag for your book. Your cover should be interesting to see and grab the reader's attention right away. The cover is the best element in designing the book. It is the first thing you see. If it does not look appealing, readers will not read it. Every cover is made differently, whether it is a picture of the author or an animated design. It does not matter what it looks like to you, but it makes a difference when you are giving the readers what they like.

Think about the setting of your story, how it looks, what the tone is, and what you want to use to symbolize your book. The cover is what makes your book unique. The reader should visualize the story from the cover. It should never lose the attention. It is your visual story. Having a front, back, and spine cover gains trust for the reader.

Book cover:

1. Determine what images and symbols describe your book.

2. Your genre

3. Will you use a photo of yourself?

4. Do you want an illustrator?

5. What colors do you want in your book?

Cover design: Front cover

1.   KDP has cover templates

2.   Must include your title (position)

3.   Subtitle

4.   Author's name

Spine cover: The title, author's name, and publisher's logo.

Back cover: (blurb). Include genre (upper right corner).

1.   Hook (above the synopsis). Is there a question or statement that makes your book stand out? Include it in a prominent font size. Explain some of the book, but leave questions to be answered from the book.

2.   Synopsis (takes up the whole page)

3.   Author photo (back left)

4.   Author bio (include bio web addresses)

5.   Barcode (the barcode purchased at Bowker—lower right-hand corner 2 by 1.2 inches)

These key factors of your book are very important if you want to sell in the marketplace. This will allow your book to have all the requirements to submit to libraries. Your book will look professional and well put together. You can hire designers on many websites like LinkedIn and more. Take a look at their previous work and determine if you would like to hire them.

Will you hire professionals to design and edit your book?

_____

_____

Budget Sheet:

Editor: $_____

Designer: $_____

Website designer: $_____

Marketing: $_____

Bank account: $_____

Business cards: $_____

ISBN: $_____

LSSN: $_____

Business structure: $_____

Distributors: $_____

Shipping: $_____

Barcodes: $_____

Expenses: $_____

Business bank account: $_____

Printing: $_____

Advertising: $_____

Business phone: $_____

Copyright registration: $_____

Tip Sheet:

- Read this book twice a day.

- Read *The Complete Guide to Self-Publishing* by Avery Cardoza.

- Visit www.bookhelpdesk.com when you are struggling.

- Select a marketable subject (nonfiction, fiction, or poetry).

- Open a business account.

- Keep track of bookkeeping.

- Write out your business plan and seek ways to gain exposure.

- Set realistic goals.

- Create a daily log so you can track progress.

- When times get hard, please remember to never give up. Keep your head up and stay focused.

- Keep going. You can achieve anything you put your mind to.

STEP 7:

PUBLISHING ON AMAZON AND MORE

When you self-publish and have your ISBN for your book, you can sell your book on any platform from which they will accept your book. Since it is registered under your company name, that is the publisher. Sign up for KDP, Kindle Direct Publishing on Amazon.

1. Set up using the ISBN you purchase; do not use the free one.

2. Do NOT choose to extend distribution.

3. Create an author page on Facebook, Instagram, Pinterest, and other platforms you choose to network from. You want people to be able to find you and when they do, they will recognize your professionalism.

4. Create an Amazon Central account to track your book sales, see reviews, fix all your book issues, and buy all your books. You can list your website, blog, and social media here, all on one page. This page is important because if you become an Amazon best seller, readers can be directed there easily on one platform.

5. Submit your edited manuscript to KDP and it will format your eBook for you. Amazon KDP will allow you to view your bookshelf, edit, and promote books. You can order author copies.

KDP will allow you to use their template to create your book. You will be able to enter your information as you go. Kindle is free to publish, but we do not want to use the free ISBN. Check out books at the bookstore to see how they look. They offer promotional deals and advertisements for your book. You will need to sign up, and your books will be on the bookshelf. After creating the account you will need to create your author page on Amazon. You can create this page on Kindle once you have signed up for an account. You will be able to order your books as well from here.

You will need to create your author page so people can locate your books directly. This will give you exposure and potential sales. This page is important because you want to have everything organized and easy for customers to find you. Once you publish on Amazon you will need to sign up with all of Amazon's sale channels to sell lots of books.

The author page needs to include:

1. Compelling bio

2. Professional author photos

3. A list of your published books

4. Book trailers and previews

5. Lead to your blog

6. Follow button

7. Your social media and website information

If you want to sell a massive number of books, you need to sell on every platform possible. IngramSpark is one of the largest book distributors in the world. They supply thousands of independent bookstores with books. Ingram is a self-publishing company that will assure you sell books. They will make sure your books are inside bookstores and market your book. You can edit your manuscript and cover on their site. You are to use the same ISBN you purchased earlier. Once you connect your company from BOWKER, you then are getting publications under your company. Ingram is a life changer. Be sure to check out all they have to offer to your company.

You will need to use the same ISBN on IngramSpark and any time you are doing anything with that one book. Using the same ISBN keeps all the sales and leads directed to one book. IngramSpark is very important, so please remember to sign up for an account to sell tons of books. Ingram will distribute and sell your books, becoming your lifetime partner.

- Order your author copies on Amazon or Ingram. They have the same quality and the price is about the same to print—approximately $2.65 per book. You will only pay the price for printing.

- While waiting on your author copies, sign up for a Shopify account. Create your online bookstore here. Get a professional web designer for better results.

- Shopify: Number 1 eCommerce platform for all types of businesses. You want to create your online bookstore.

- When you start promoting your book you want to promote your website so that readers can connect directly to you.

- You keep more money when customers buy directly from you.

- Audiobook: If you want to make your book into an audio version, go to ACX.com using your Amazon login from your Amazon Central account. ACX is Amazon's company that produces audiobooks. This version is helpful for readers who cannot read or don't have the time to read.

- If you want to record yourself, you will need:

1. MV-88 microphone and iPhone.

2. Audio engineer to clean up the audio.

3. Edit regarding ACX requirements.

You want to have a web designer design your website for the best results. You will be able to link all of your social media accounts to your website. The more channels and leads you have, the more sales you can obtain. Facebook is the leading source on social media sites and popular for mobile activities. Use Facebook to create another author page like the Amazon APP. Facebook will allow you to connect all other accounts and verify that you sell on their platform. Once you are clear to sell there, it automatically qualifies for other channels through Facebook. Always remember, the more people who can see your book the better.

STEP 8:

PROMOTE UNTIL YOU CAN'T ANYMORE

Pitch your book to independent bookstores:

1. Find your local bookstores on www.indiebound.org

2. Bookstores: www.booklocker.com

www.borders.com

www.ebookmall.com

3. Always check the submission guidelines.

4. Pitch for shelf space and decide whether you are wanting to do a book signing at that bookstore.

5. You want to describe why your book needs space and why it will be a good fit.

6. You want to make sure your proposal is professional and imposing.

Submit a query letter to sell nonfiction books. This should include what you have to offer and what you are seeking. Create your target market plan. Conduct market research with race, gender, and age.

Market analysis:

1. Target your ideal audience.

2. Determine your location.

3. Determine how responsive the market is.

Hosting a book signing is a great way to interact with your customers and sign books. You can submit a proposal to the local bookstores where you would like to sign your books. You will need to organize your press kit so it will deliver the same results.

A press kit includes:

1. Your book brochure

2. Reviews

3. Press release

4. Business cards

5. Biographic information

6. Interview questions

7. Book tour dates

8. Copies of books

Create a press email because you need to have a certain team handling the press. Collect addresses, names, and emails for the mailing list. Submit press releases to radio and podcast stations. Reach out to reporters to do a story on you and your book. Your marketing has to be consistent and you have to be patient to see results. You can search promotion sites, but here are some ideas:

- Groundwork

- Special events

- Flyers

- Book listings

- Yellow pages

- Interviews
- Post signs in stores
- Ads
- Referrals
- Churches

What makes your book marketable?

_____

_____

_____

What are the goals you want to achieve as an author?

_____

_____

_____

Poetry Motivation

My dreams were never dreams,

But an alert for what was soon to be.

If you can believe it, you will only receive it.

Never let your dreams sit.

You have a message to inspire,

No matter the process, you will not quit.

You have come this far because you can feel it in your spirit,

Believe it! You can do it!

Take your time and relax your mind,

Use God's gift and always be kind.

For this guide will lead you in the right direction,

Take action and work to reach your destination.

Commit to your goal and pray throughout the day,

For He will not forsake you and He will lead the way.

No matter the pain,

Never give up, try your best to maintain.

The darkest hour is close to day,

Remember you are always safe.

You can fulfill any dream in your life journey,

Move at your own pace.

Life is not a race,

Chase your goals and you will never run out of space.

Everything will flow at ease, like a river wave,

Never complicate life for you can have it your way.

Write down the information you gathered from the previous steps. This area is for you to organize your book niche, message, and goals to start your publishing journey.

More notes:

STEP 9:

TIMING AND STRUCTURE

Timing is very important when releasing a book. You want to have quality in your work so that it will hold value. You may want to hurry and release it because the topic is hot, but that will not produce the best result. Set your book goals promptly. Find your professional editor to edit and proofread your book so you don't sound completely like an idiot. They should look for typos and grammatical errors. The designer should design the interior so that it will be easy to read and clear for the eyes. You want to send it to a few people to see if your story is flowing correctly. You do not want your book to sound choppy when someone is reading it. This will help your book sell because people can rely on credible correct work rather than sloppy all-over-the-place projects. You want to give yourself one month or more to have this step completed by two or more editors to ensure the quality is good. The more organized with your time you are, the better results you'll see. This is the best way you can get a lot of work done. You want to keep in mind your budget and find freelancers to help create the book. Set deadlines when you start writing your book.

How to stay on track:

1. Write down your daily goals and tasks. Items on your list will get done faster if you write them down. If you have a goal to complete every day, you are being productive. You want to use your time wisely.

2. Determine how long you are going to work on your book each day. This will keep you on the road to success. Tests show that keeping up with your writing makes the process more exciting. You may learn new things as you write, so do not

rush your thoughts. The more time spent on a project, the better the outcome.

3.   Maintain organization. This is the biggest key to self-publishing your book. You hold many responsibilities, so it is important you have everything organized. As the accountant, you want to make sure bank accounts are linked to all platforms sold on. As the creator, you want to have all supporting documentation of proposals, receipts, etc. from the editors and designers you hired.

4.   Identify your strengths and weaknesses. You need to understand that if you are not good at concentrating, you need to find a way to be able to concentrate well. Use your strongest areas to help your weakest ones.

5.   Set deadlines. For every goal there should be a deadline. This makes it visible for you to see as you work. Being aware of the time used and the time left is important to the brain. It will trigger your brain to get the job done within the deadline you wrote down.

Daily Goal:

Five action steps to achieve goal

1.

2.

3.

4.

5.

Five obstacles you are facing

1.

2.

3.

4.

5.

Deadline:

Extra notes:

Daily Action Sheet:

Daily Goal:
Five action steps to achieve goal 1. 2. 3. 4. 5.
Five obstacles you are facing 1. 2. 3. 4. 5.
Deadline:
Extra notes:

Daily Goal:

Five action steps to achieve goal

1.

2.

3.

4.

5.

Five obstacles you are facing

1.

2.

3.

4.

5.

Deadline:

Extra notes:

Daily Goal:

Five action steps to achieve goal

1.

2.

3.

4.

5.

Five obstacles you are facing

1.

2.

3.

4.

5.

Deadline:

Extra notes:

Daily Goal:

Five action steps to achieve goal

1.

2.

3.

4.

5.

Five obstacles you are facing

1.

2.

3.

4.

5.

Deadline:

Extra notes:

STEP 10:
RELEASING

No one cares if you think your book is good, that is why you have to show them why your book is the best. You are an expert at what you are writing about. Make sure your confidence is high to deliver your message strongly. You have to be able to answer all the questions about your book that people may have. Make sure the problem you are solving for your readers is clear. People only want to buy what they can benefit from. You must know your market like an expert. You must be clear on your marketing plan and releasing plan. Before you release your book, you want to plan your release. Write a book publicity plan. This blueprint for success helps you decide strategies and tactics to reach your goal. Your plan needs to be straightforward and simple. This is important even if your book has been out for some time.

Your publicity plan should include:

1. The situation or overview

2. Review of the audience being targeted

3. Your goals you want to achieve

4. The objectives

5. Strategies you have

6. Tactics you have

7. Your overall budget

8. A timeline with all your dates and times.

1. Describe what makes your book different from your competitors:

- What makes your book marketable?

- Include your unique credentials.

- Include any social media interviews you took part in.

- What makes you a marketable author?

2. Target your audience:

- Who will buy your book?

- What media outlets are you going to use?

- What makes it marketable?

- Are they effective?

- Who do you want to read your books?

- What age group do you want to write for?

3. Goals:

- How much money do you want to make?

- How much money do you want to use for marketing?

- Budget.

- Your intention.

- What are your main reasons for selling your books?

- How and why do you want to make an impact?

1. Objectives include:

- Targets with deadlines.

- You want to be very specific on your goals: you want to address how you can achieve that goal in your objectives.

- Expected accomplishments.

- Who will do the work to make sure you succeed?

- When will it be finished?

- How do you know your goal has been achieved?

- How are you going to make book sales?

2. Strategies include:

- Where customers can buy your books.

- How can you market your book in your intended marketplace?

- Are you using paid promotions?

- How do you want to connect with potential customers?

- What can you do to make more sales?

- How can you make an income and an impact?

- Provide how you will accumulate sales.

- Provide the platforms you want to use as channels.

- Any strategies you can use to gain sales, either indirectly or directly.

3. Tactics:

- What are you going to do to get publicity?

- Tangible.

- Press releases.

- Bylined articles.

- Virtual book tours.

- Press kits.

4. Budget:

- Budget from what you can afford from your tactics.

- How much you want to spend versus how much you will need to spend.

- You will always need to know your budget.

- Budget first before you start the process.

5. Timeline:

- Timeline helps manage tactics and tasks.

- You need to know your start and end date for promotions.

- Set deadlines for press releases.

- Set a deadline for your pre-order and release date.

- Deadline for publicity plan.

- A timeline is important if you want to stay organized.

- Write down tactics and objectives that will help market your book.

When you are releasing your book, you need to:

- Develop your book message to the media.

- Deliver a clear message every time you communicate with the media.

- Communicate the most important/main message you want to give.

- Include your supporting information, statistics, etc.

Create a press page for your site and include:

1. Where books can be purchased

2. Highlights

3. Book announcement

4. Author bio

5. Book cover

6. Q&A

7. Tip sheets

8. Sample book review

Announce your book press release:

1. What is the release date?

2. Create a new email for the press to submit inquiries to reporters.

3. Write an attention-grabbing headline.

4. Describe your book.

5. The first to third paragraphs of your release should answer the WHO, WHAT, WHEN, WHERE, WHY, AND HOW.

6. Be professional.

FIRST PARAGRAPH:

1. Does your lead say what the release is about?

2. Start broad and get specific later in the release.

3. What are key facts about the book?

SECOND PARAGRAPH:

1. More detail.

2. Introduce the title and author name.

3. Anything else that readers need to know.

THIRD PARAGRAPH:

1. More details about the book.

2. What is special about the book?

3. What makes your book different?

4. Include a quote of why you wrote the book and why it's useful.

5. Include your credentials (who you are and your connection).

6. Conclude as to where they can buy your book.

Press distribution services where you can send your press release range from paid releases to free releases. This is important because this can drive backlink traffic to your book.

No charge services:

Https://www.vitispr.com/

Https://www.prweb.com/

Https://www.expertclick.com

www.dreams-unlimited.com

www.lisawrites.com

www.quality-books.com

www.about-books.com

You can promote on promotional sites by simply Googling "book promotion sites." Promotion sites help target your book to book readers.

https://www.pr.com/promote-your-business/

– offers both free and paid promotions.

When you are releasing your press release, it is also important to create an Author Q&A. Questions and answers will prepare you for radio interviews. You need to know exactly who you are going to be sending the release to: radio, TV, daily newspapers, etc. Press is the way to get your book out there. Since no one knows you yet it is important. After reaching out to reporters, get interview questions together. Every time you are talking to the press you should have the same answer. Keep your reason for writing clear. This is very important to interacting with the press. You will need press to sell a massive amount of books.

Here are some sample questions to help with interviews:

1.   Why did you write the book?

2.   What will surprise the readers most about your book?

3.   What surprised you while writing?

4.   What's the most important message?

5.   Did writing the book save your life?

6.   What are your hopes for readers?

7.   What are you working on now?

Think of questions that people might want to ask you but cannot reach you. Tip sheets are also important when you are releasing. They are specific types of PR that offer tips in bullet point form. Tip sheets are best used for news briefs or magazine articles. Tip sheets include the main advice for readers. This valuable tool is useful for nonfiction authors.

- Reviews are important because they give your book credit. The more your book is in the media the better. You can write an editorial review in your Amazon account. You want to write an unbiased review but sound like your biggest fan. You are writing an editorial review so that you can spark it up. The review needs to be objective and positive, of course. Journalists and interviewers check your reviews to form your interview.

- A book review has an introduction, discussion, and conclusion. It should be 700–1,000 words. The shorter the better.

- Heading: Include book title, author, publisher, and publication date.

- Discussion: Include thoughts about the book. Ask whether it made the correct impact as intended.

- Fiction or nonfiction: Include if the story is nonfiction or fiction.

- Conclusion: Should be strong and include why you wrote the book and the solution you use to solve the problem you are addressing.

Media list:
- LinkedIn
- Https://www.vsnpl.com/
- Https://www.radioslocator.com/
- Podcast

- Article syndication sites

- Inbound.org

- Medium

- Slideshare

- Quora

- Outbrain

- Taboola

- Scoop it

- Reddit

- Tumblr

- Facebook business

- www.writesweekly.com

All these media outlets will give you great results. You have to keep the buzz going after you release the book. So, submitting your book to one of these will be important for exposure. The more your book is in the media, the more books you can sell.

How to make your book interesting to buy?

- Create a sound bite phrase.

- A sound bite phrase is a catchy statement that describes your book.

- Include repetition, alliteration, clever turn, and/or common phrases.

- Use memorable images.

- Release your first press release introducing your book and solutions.

Second press release:

1. Include any awards you have received after two weeks.

2. Place a thank-you note on the back of the book.

3. Set up advertising on Amazon.

Amazon advertising will allow you to create custom ads:

1. Create your Amazon ad account and product page.

2. The product page should be descriptive, contain high-quality images, useful information, and support claims made in the ad.

3. Promoted ad under KDP.

4. Choose the ad type, sponsored products, and lock screen ads.

5. Sponsored products are targeted by keywords or products. They will appear within the search results.

6. Lockscreen ads are for eBooks only. They are pay-per-click targeted to appear on the Kindle E-reader tablet lock screen.

7. Create your ad, making sure it includes all requirements.

8. Submit for an ad review – it can take 72 hours

9. www.google.com/adwords

10. www.facebook.com/advertising

11. business.instagram.com/advertising

12. ads.twitter.com

The key to running successful ads are keywords and targeting the right customers. Start with a small budget and then increase. This is why it is important to know your target audience. You can include this in your marketing plan. How are you going to reach customers?

Determine your targeted audience and your why.

_____

_____

_____

_____

_____

Why is your solution needed?

_____

_____

_____

_____

_____

What problem are you solving with your book?

_____

_____

_____

_____

_____

STEP 11:

LIFE AFTER THE RELEASE

Robert Kiyosaki has been quoted as saying, "I'm not a best-writing author, I'm a best-selling author." It does not matter if you are a bad writer. You can sell a large number of books with the steps I provided. It does not matter what your book is about or even if it is good. It needs to have some value though to make an impact. Content is king and that is the way you keep the reader's attention. Customers need to be excited before and after the book release. The plan is to have pre-orders before the release date. You need to always reference your book in your daily life. You are the marketing machine, so make people fall in love with you. If they love you, they will love everything you do. If people love you, then they will trust whatever you deliver. Once you gain trust in your audience, you gain great reviews.

After you release your book you want to keep track of your analytics. Be mindful of how many channels you are using to sell your book. Come up with a promotional plan so that you can always promote your book. Test different strategies and grow your audience. After you release you want to keep the buzz going as long as you can. The more people who see your book, the more people you can impact.

If you are an aspiring author, these steps are critical for your career. I'll say that, from experience, if you skip a step, you will not see the results you intend. You must be fully committed to the publishing process if you want to self-publish. I believe in you and your vision. Your story is needed on the market. Make sure you're an expert with your solution. It is your time to take full control of your dream.

Notes:

Notes:

Read more books by me (Inspired by K: An Inspirational Chapbook – book of poems).

Every poem is designed to give off positive vibrations as you read. Every poem is written to inspire you to live and think more positively. After reading, you will feel good and enlightened. You will receive positive changes in your life.

Please pre-order this children's book written by me: The ABCs and 123s of Animals, Colors, and More which will be released the summer of 2021.

This book is for kids ages two through five. Children will learn their alphabet, numbers, colors, vegetables, and more. It is easy for beginners to learn. It has lots of activities to keep the kids engaged in reading.

Services offered by Kenshae:

- Big sister program which provides little sisters with emotional support. Meets with the little sister weekly to talk about goals, school, and more. She will help young ladies if they need financial assistance.

- Speaking engagements start at $100 per hour.

- Self-publishing coaching: teaches and guides aspiring authors one on one, working with their manuscript and helping them throughout the process. Fee starts at $500.

Made in the USA
Monee, IL
15 September 2021